It's Easier To Give Birth Than Resurrect The Dead

A Proactive Approach to

Managing Employees

Ted Duboise

Ted Duboise

Published by On Point! Publishers

ISBN: 0615882102
ISBN-13: 978-0615882109

DEDICATION

This book is dedicated to the memory of Joe Elmore. It is because of his training that this book is possible.

Ted Duboise

CONTENTS

Ted Duboise

ACKNOWLEDGMENTS

This book would not have been possible without the support and encouragement of my wife, Pam Duboise.

During my career in the restaurant business, I have met and worked with numerous managers. One that I will always remember was a man named Joe Elmore. I worked for Joe only six months but he taught me the most about interviewing and hiring employees!

PART I
Ressurecting the Dead

CHAPTER 1

DEADBEAT WORKERS

Haley just arrived at work. It's 2:03 pm. Haley was scheduled to be at work at 2:00 pm. As soon as Haley got inside the restaurant, she headed to the restroom to get her make-up in order.

By the time she got her make-up right, put her apron on, and picked up her order book, Haley made it to her work station at 2:27 pm. Just a typical start to her shift at Donna's Deli.

Donna, the owner, spoke to Haley as she arrived. "Glad you made it", Donna told her. "We've been busy all day. Mr. Johnson has already been seated in your station. He wants his 'usual'. Be sure to check the special board."

Donna never mentioned to Haley that she was late. Not as she arrived and not at the end of Haley's shift.

Deadbeat workers are a given. They're out there. Are they working for you?

"It's Easier To Give Birth Than Resurrect The Dead" is a Proactive Approach to Deadbeat Employees, based on 30 years of experience in the restaurant industry.

The precepts outlined here are not "academic theory". They are real-life! These systems and processes have been proven in several restaurant concepts through the years.

How Do Deadbeats Get In Your Staff?

Deadbeat employees creep into your operation undetected. Why and How? Because you hired them! That person went through your interview process and you gave them a job. You put him/her to work. You issue that person a paycheck just the same as you pay everyone else on your staff.

And yet, you know that he/she does not perform just the same as everyone else. What's worse, everyone on your staff knows that this person does not perform. By paying the deadbeat the same as the rest of your staff, you are being unfair to your entire crew.

It is unfair for everyone else to do most of the work and the deadbeat still draws the same pay. Furthermore, the deadbeat gets the same benefits including medical insurance.

So why do you/me/we keep the deadbeat worker on our payroll? How did he/she get hired?

Let's answer the second question first. There are usually two reasons that you have a deadbeat employee:
1. You made a mistake in hiring.
2. You inherited the person when you assumed responsibility for a different unit or department.

In either case, the deadbeat has survived thus far. They will continue to survive until you, as the manager, "Take Action". If you made a mistake in hiring, admit it (to yourself), and take action. If you inherited the deadbeat, take action.

Take Action means:
Do your best to change the employee into a productive worker or do them a favor and free up the future of that person. If you can't enhance that person's life, then let someone else give it a try.

Remember, deadbeats survive – but only if allowed. This step, "Take Action" will be discussed in detail in a later chapter.

Now, to answer the first question, "Why do we keep the deadbeat?"

Well, as for yourself, you'll have to answer that. Everyone has his/her own reason(s) for keeping deadbeat employees. In most every case, we make excuses for our own lack of action. Really, there is no excuse. We convince ourselves with thoughts like, "Oh, he is trying hard." Or "She does the best she can."

You are in denial. You are the one that can change this situation. Do not tolerate deadbeat employees!

Free up their future and let them work somewhere else where the standards are low or non-existent. Why?

Among other things, deadbeats kill morale of the rest of the staff; they kill productivity which cost money for the business; and they cause other employees to leave your business which will cost your business more money to hire and train new employees.

Let's discuss some of these problems.

.

CHAPTER 2

7 TRAITS OF A DEADBEAT

Jeremy is a cook at Donna's Deli. An employee at the Deli for almost two years, Jeremy has become a sort of 'key employee' for Donna. With the ebb and flow of business, typical in a restaurant, staff levels are adjusted according to the sales volume. Some employees only get part-time hours. However, Jeremy always gets a full-time schedule.

Jeremy is always late for work. Sometimes, he arrives as much as thirty minutes past his scheduled start time. He may be clean-shaven or not and his uniform is not always up to par. The food that he cooks is sometimes over-cooked and sloppily prepared.

Many times, he doesn't re-stock his station at the end of his shift, leaving more work for his fellow employees. Occasionally, he leaves work early, putting even more work on his teammates.

Donna overlooks Jeremy's errors because of his tenure with her. "Even though Jeremy is late to work, I know that I can depend on him to be here," said Donna. "You just don't know how hard it is to get good employees around here."

Many managers fail to see the big picture with deadbeat employees. Donna, and many managers like her, will justify the deadbeat's existence. Management's failure to take action allows the deadbeat to live on.

Three Effects of Deadbeats:

1. Deadbeats kill morale
2. Deadbeats kill productivity
3. Deadbeats cause employee turnover

Let's talk about these and explore their effects.

Deadbeats Kill Morale

Employees want to be able to work in a place where co-workers strive to achieve the same goals. They want to come to work and do their part along with their teammates. Workers want to feel that the boss is pleased with their work and really cares about the job he or she does.

When there is a deadbeat among them, and no action is taken to correct the situation, other employees get the opinion that the boss doesn't care.

Why should they work hard? Jeremy doesn't work hard, is always late for work, and he gets away with it. Haley is never reprimanded for tardiness and still gets the best station in the house.

Deadbeats kill the spirit of the workers in a unit or department.

Deadbeats Kill Productivity

In any business, staff members must be efficient. Quality work is essential for any business to succeed. If employees aren't productive the business will experience payroll costs that are higher than they should be.

A business with high labor cost will ultimately have to increase the selling price of their products – not a good thing in today's business climate. Consumers expect quality products at low prices.

In the restaurant business, labor cost is the second highest expense on the P & L. The restaurant business is also speed-intensive. Products must be prepared and delivered quickly or customers will go to another restaurant. Loss of sales will cause the business to have less payroll dollars available. The amount of labor dollars you have to spend on payroll is budgeted on forecasted sales. If the sales do not materialize, then you have less money to pay employees.

Deadbeat workers are not fast workers. They don't produce as many hamburgers as needed and many burgers must be re-made because they are not made as ordered by the customer.

Here is an example of productivity loss. At one restaurant I managed, the standard productivity rate for one cook was $55 per man hour. We knew that, given the menu we had at that time, one cook could produce $55 worth of food per hour. Our payroll was budgeted at that number. So if we had a cook that couldn't match that productivity rate, we knew that we would blow budgeted payroll.

Deadbeats "ride" the clock without getting their work completed, leaving many of their duties to be completed by co-workers.

Deadbeats Cause Good Employees To Quit

Most employee teams are eager to meet production rates and quotas. They want to keep the boss happy. However, with a laggard team member, those production quotas can't be met. Good employees will work harder or longer just to meet the quotas and take up the slack of the deadbeat employee.

But the good employee will only keep up this pace for a short period of time. Eventually, he/she will look to the boss to take action. If supervisors take no action with the deadbeat employee, the good team members will simply find another job.

In spite of the economy, good jobs will be easily found by good workers.

So how can you spot a deadbeat employee? How can a supervisor know that this person that he/she hired or inherited is a deadbeat? Identifying a deadbeat is usually just a matter of observing the performance of your staff. Measure performance against company benchmarks. Maybe the deadbeat often leaves work earlier than the scheduled-out time and skipped out on the end-of-shift duties.

Of course, your other staff members will let you know, but you, as the supervisor should not wait until other staff members come to you complaining about another employee. Here are seven traits that I have identified as the mark of deadbeat employees.

7 Traits of a Deadbeat Employee:

1. Always tardy, no matter the scheduled time.
2. Cannot keep pace with the work load demand.
3. High rate of workmanship defects
4. Continuously complains about job, rules, other employees
5. Always has excuses for not completing job duties
6. Criticizes the company, its products, staff
7. Takes shortcuts rather than follow company procedures

Do you have a staff member that fits this description? Then it's time to fix the problem. There is a solution.

Why do many managers fail to take action against deadbeat employees? Most managers do not want to face conflict. Reprimanding an employee could possibly cause conflict. However, if each employee is held to the standards of the unit each shift, conflict will not arise very often.

CHAPTER 3

WE'RE IN THE PEOPLE BUSINESS, PEOPLE

In my years of operating businesses, I have learned many keys to being successful. I have learned systems, processes and best practices. No matter the type business or the type of industry, there must be systems and procedures in place to operate successfully. Whether it's manufacturing, retail, customer service, or academic, operating procedures will vary – some more detailed than others. The equipment and tools will be the same in some businesses but different in other businesses.

Amongst the systems, equipment and tools, I have found that there is one common denominator in business and industry: *people*. It takes *people* to make all of it work! Learning this one essential key has bode me well through the years.

I'm sure that you have seen the slogan, "People are our most valuable asset". Indeed, people are assets – but people are more than that. They are not "just" an asset.

Whether it's manufacturing, retail, customer service, or academic, it takes *people* to create and execute the systems, policies and procedures. There may be computers and robots to do some of the production work and to automate production. But it takes *people* to sell the finished product.

I have yet to hear about a computer calling up another computer and placing an order for more widgets – unless a human executed the command or programmed the computer to place the order automatically at certain inventory levels. A human had to decide at what level of inventory would trigger the computer to place the order. The order is for tried and proven products. New ideas must be sold by a human!

It takes people to run machines to manufacture products. It takes people to run machines that deliver those products (planes, trains, trucks). It takes people to run machines that ring up your purchases of those products. Simply put, "It takes people!"

No matter what business you are in, you must have *people* to be a success. You may be the sole employee but you need *people* to sell you products for resell and you need *people* to buy your product. If your business grows and you decide to expand, then you recruit *people* to work with you. Now, you have employees (people), co-worker *people* and customer *people*.

It's *all* about the *people*. How you treat your *people* and how your *people* treat *people* is the one true factor in the success of any business or even in life in general.

We are in the *people* business no matter what product or service we sell. Learn how to deal with *people* and you will be a success.

Why is it relevant to understand that we're in the people business? Simple answer. That deadbeat worker is *people*, too! Since people is our business, how you handle the deadbeat worker situation will be crucial to maintaining respect with your staff.

Your staff will be watching what you do, for several reasons. First, they want to solve the situation without putting more workload on them. They are tired of dealing with the deadbeat but they need a team member to help them meet production quotas.

Second, they will observe how you handle that person in relation to their work experience. The question in all of their minds: will the way you solve the problem make their jobs harder, easier, or about the same?

Some employees may not see the person as a deadbeat. They are this person's friend and are sympathetic to him/her. They may feel that you are handling the situation wrong.

Deadbeats are people and have feelings too. Therefore, dealing with a deadbeat should be approached from a people standpoint. We want to solve the situation but with the respect and dignity that all people deserve. We also want to ensure that the approach is fair and equal, just the same as the approach we take with any employee who has to be disciplined.

In the next three chapters, we will discuss ways to revive the deadbeat and to "resurrect the dead". This is never an easy task but, since deadbeats are people too, we must give it our best shot at salvaging this person if possible.

This person at least deserves the opportunity to change, especially since we, the supervisor, must share in the responsibility for the deadbeat worker's performance. After all, we have let this person become what he/she is because we haven't tried to rehabilitate him/her.

We haven't taken the initiative to enforce, or make him/her comply with, company policies and processes.

You see, I am convinced that every business that I managed was successful because of people. I am a firm believer that my employees are Number 1 in my business. Not the customer! My employees!

I believe that if you have a happy employee, he/she will make a happy customer!

After about ten years in operating businesses, I learned this concept that, "We are in the people business". Since that time, my philosophy and business practices have all been rolled up into these two tenets:

1. Have more people than necessary available,
2. Ensure that those people receive the ultimate Guest Service, higher than my customers.

I know that many of you - no, most of you - will have a hard time grasping this idea. You will never be as successful as you could be until you ingrain this philosophy into your very soul!

I will leave it at that. I'm not going to preach to you, but for the last twenty years, I have proven this works for me.

In short, it works like this:
- Hire more people than you need because you will need them at some point – and you will be ready when that need arises
- Reward your people with the greatest work atmosphere that they will ever be privileged to work in; praise them for work well done – every time; thank them for every positive achievement; treat them with the utmost respect and ensure that everyone else does the same.

"It doesn't matter what product you make or sell, you are in the _people_ business!"

CHAPTER 4

EMPLOYEE REVIEW
IS YOUR REVIEW

A formal employee performance review or evaluation is a crucial part of employee life. Staff members want to know, on a regular basis, how he/she rates in the boss' eye.

If you are getting ready to do an employee review, consider this:

When you perform an employee review, you are actually doing your own review.

As you complete each item, goal or result, consider what _you_ did to make that employee better in that area. Or, consider what you didn't do that could have made the employee achieve better results.

Ultimately, the buck stops with you. Ponder the following:
1) Did you give specific, clear goals?
2) Did you set a time deadline for the result to be achieved?
3) Did you give critical and timely feedback as necessary?
4) Did you train, teach and coach the person?
5) Did you hold that employee accountable to the goals that were set?

Notice that in every question, there is the word "you". You, as the supervisor, are responsible and accountable for the actions and performance of your employees. Therefore, just remember, that when you do an employee review, you are doing your own review.

The employee's strengths and weaknesses are whatever that you have coached him/her on the past three months. How do you rate?

In many companies, formal employee reviews are completed every six months or once each year. Typically, the company has a standard form that is used with every employee in an effort to be consistent and fair throughout the employee ranks. However, do not just give grades. There must be conversation and interaction with the employee. He/she must have input. A review is a two-way conversation.

In my opinion, this frequency is fine with managers and supervisors. However, I do not believe that it is right frequency for hourly staff. I believe that formal reviews for hourly employees must occur at a minimum of every three months to be effective.

To be successful, a formal hourly review must accomplish the following:

- Recap the employee's achievements during the past three months, especially noting strengths and weaknesses in the skills that the employee utilizes in the day-to-day performance of his/her duties
- Note special accomplishments by the employee along with special commendations
- Attendance record must be noted along with tardiness and times when employee stayed late to finish a project or to help in other areas of the business
- Be honest! Be straightforward. Don't sugar-coat. The employee must know the truth
- Plans to further develop the employees weaknesses and to utilize the employee's strengths
- Goals must be set for the next three months. Be specific, very clear of the expectations.

A review should never be a surprise. In other words, the employee should never be surprised by a note or comment by the supervisor. If a supervisor has done a good job for the last three months in communicating with that employee, he/she will already know the outcome of the review. It is just a "process" to make the review formal.

The way to never have a surprise during a formal review is daily feedback. Employee development is most effective if feedback from the supervisor occurs every shift or at least two-three times weekly.

Daily coaching lets the employee know exactly what is expected and what the boss is wanting to see. Employees who receive immediate feedback (positive or negative) will have an overall better performance than someone who never receives any type of coaching or feedback – (maybe your deadbeat employee?).

Keep notes of those daily coaching sessions in a file for future reference. You will pull those out for the formal review process and use them to give an accurate assessment of that employees skills, accomplishments, strengths and weakness.

Teachable Moments

I was the Sr. Kitchen Manager for three years at an Italian restaurant. As each recipe was made, we had the cook taste the finished recipe. By doing this, the cook would know precisely what that recipe should taste like, along with the texture and consistency of the final product.

One day I came into work just before lunch. My lead cook, Jason, had opened the kitchen that day. As I made my way through the kitchen, as usual, I was tasting final products. I discovered a sauce that had an ingredient missing. I went to Jason and had him taste the sauce. He quickly agreed that the sauce was missing an ingredient. When asked how this occurred, he stated that one of the other cooks had actually made the sauce.

This was a great time for what I call a "Teachable Moment". I got together Jason and the other cook and we began tasting the sauce and trying to figure out the missing ingredient.

When pressed, the other cook couldn't remember if he had put in the black pepper. In my taste tests, I was fairly certain that the black pepper was the item. We added some black pepper and, sure enough, it was the missing ingredient.

I reviewed with both cooks how imperative it was to follow the recipe precisely. Had I not done my job and taste-tested the batches of sauces, our customers would have received an inferior product. An inconsistent menu item will eventually turn your customers to other items and could possibly lead to that customer patronizing your competitors.

Teachable Moments occur every day in your operation. Seize the moment and train that employee. Not only train them in the correct procedure or process, but teach them the "why" that the procedure must be done this way – and the same way every time.

One of my favorite analogies is Coca-Cola. Everyone knows what it tastes like. If you don't like the taste, then don't buy it. But one thing is for certain: if you buy it you will know what you are getting because every bottle taste the same.

A restaurant should be the same. When you put an item on the menu, then that item must taste the same every time. The customer will know exactly what they are getting if they decide to buy that item. If that recipe is made with an ingredient missing, then you have cheated the customer. They didn't get what they paid for.

Utilize Teachable Moments when they occur. Many times they will occur unexpectedly. You have to be able to recognize that moment.

"An employee review should never be a surprise to the employee!"

CHAPTER 5

DEADBEAT DEVELOPMENT

Now, let's move on to resurrecting the dead. I must warn you now. This plan, or any plan, may not work. There is no guarantee. Sometimes, no matter the energy and time put into turning around a laggard employee, no plan of any kind will work and you will have to free-up the future of that person. Set'em free. Free up their future and let them work somewhere else where the standards are low or non-existent.

Now, understand that I am not advocating the wholesale firing of low-performing employees. To the contrary, I feel it is a manager's duty to do all that can be done to improve every employee's performance.

I have been involved with the turnaround of both hourly employees and with management employees. In one company, I was the resident turnaround manager. Any non-performing manager was sent to my district to change them. If they didn't perform after working in my district, we would free up his/her future.

I think that one of the key things to remember in this situation, is this employee usually has a family. When the livelihood is gone, he/she not only loses a paycheck but also the benefits that went along with the job. Most employers now offer insurance benefits, even to part-timers, and medical insurance is critical in many cases.

So we don't just develop a turn-around plan without the input from the employee. As a supervisor, before the development meeting, you need to set out the guidelines of the plan and what goals must be accomplished. Then, with the employee, finalize the overall strategy for success.

Creating a Formal Development Plan

I feel that the first step in creating a formal development plan is to do a performance review. As with any development plan, you must know strengths and weaknesses of the employee. If the employee already works with you, then you'll know more about the person. If it is a person that you inherited or was sent to you for development, the review process will help both of you to learn more about each other.

I would suggest to hold two separate meetings; the first for the performance review and a later meeting to discuss the development plan. You will create a better development plan after going through the performance review.

I would also highly suggest that you confer with other management personnel about this person's performance and get their input on how they see this person. They can give you their view of what the person needs to be focused on, which will help you develop a better plan. The entire management team will be a part of this person's development and follow-up so they need to be privy to expectations.

The Development Plan Meeting

Set the meeting date and time where you are free to focus with no or very little interruptions. This is a very important meeting (just like with your boss), so make it a convenient time for both of you.

You must put the employee at ease. Get him/her to open up to you and discuss what he/she has in mind for the job. Make the person understand that this meeting and development plan is for them to succeed and that you, as the supervisor, and the rest of the managers are committed to the plan for his/her success.

Be candid in your conversation with the employee. Establish clear and specific expectations. If you have an understanding now, there will be no misunderstanding later.

Outline the actions that must happen first, next, and so on.

Action Steps in Development Plan:

1. Performance Review
2. Discuss, determine strengths, weaknesses, skillsets. Determine activities to utilize strengths, develop weaknesses
3. Determine if employee needs to work with a skill trainer, if so, how long and what outcome is expected
4. Should the person review company training videos and manuals, possibly take and pass training exams again
5. Set benchmarks to be attained and in what time frame, e.g., company production standards must be met four of five shifts
6. Set deadlines for any reports or tests to be due
7. Establish follow-up times, i.e. weekly, bi-weekly or monthly
8. Set up next review period, date for next performance review
9. Establish the role of the supervisor in the plan, what he/she will do to ensure employee gets the help and has the tools necessary for success of the development plan
10. Follow-up each day, discuss results immediately with the deadbeat, coach the person on what needs to happen.

The Final Review

At the next review, you will check to ensure that all performance criteria and deadlines that were established in the Development Plan have been met, as assigned, and on time. Discuss any item that was not achieved.

The next step is to make a decision. Based on accomplishments, you must decide if you will continue the development or cut your losses.

Based on our "People Business" criteria, did you and your management team do all that you could possibly do? Did you make it a priority to help the person, as planned?

If everything has been done according to plan, then free up the deadbeat's future and let's move on. Resurrecting the dead is not easy.

This page was left blank intentionally.

Make notes and consider what we've covered in PART I.

PART II
Giving Birth

CHAPTER 6

TAKE ACTION

Now, let's discuss how to prevent deadbeat employees. Oh! Trust me. You will still hire deadbeats, but they will never impact your business. Why? Because you will detect them quickly and they'll be gone soon thereafter. They won't stay long.

As mentioned in a previous chapter, I was always aggressively hiring new employees. In fact, I actually had one boss tell me to quit hiring because I had so many people. However, I still made my labor budget. By having so many people, it actually made it easier to achieve my payroll budget.

My standard for staffing was to maintain 120% of my staffing needs. So if I needed 80 employees, I hired, trained, and had 98 people ready to go.

I also created an atmosphere where my restaurant was the place to work. The restaurant was popular with the locals. It was busy on weekdays and absolutely packed on weekends. I paid the cooks good money, and my wait staff made good money in tips. It was not unusual for a server to make $500-$600 per week – and worked only 30-35 hours per week.

My employees were treated as if they owned the place. Employees made their own work schedule. My rule was that if one requested a day off or a week off, that request was granted automatically – no questions asked – even if it was a weekend. In most restaurants, a weekend off for an employee might occur once or twice per year! I had one employee that took one year off and came back the next year. He wanted to go to a technical school in Florida to become a professional sound engineer. We made it happen.

Opportunity to advance within the company? Excellent. During my first seven years with that company I had a total of 15 employees promoted into management. In an industry where the annual turnover rate approaches 300%, my turnover rate was 88% annually.

How do you get so many good employees?

I've actually had my competition ask me this question! First and foremost, I have a plan. Second, I have a system. By having a plan, I know what I need at all times. Through the system, I am always looking for that great person.

If an applicant comes in and I feel that this would be a good worker, I will hire them even when I don't need anyone. I'm not about to let that person go get a job with the competition. In my business, I know that I will need that good candidate sooner or later. Does it work? If you make it work!

Here, we will discuss the plan. In the next chapter, we will discuss the system.

The Staffing Plan

Let's face it: you have a lot to do to run your business on a daily basis. And those daily tasks are a lot easier if you have quality people to help. You may not need to hire someone every week, but you do need to know when there is a possibility that you will need to fill a position. How do you know? Easy. You have a plan!

It's called a staffing plan. A staffing plan plots out the amount of staff that you will need for each position of the business. The staffing plan can be created for whatever time frame desirable. It needs to be for at least a three-month period, but can be for a longer time.

The staffing plan is a chart with weekly projected or forecasted sales over the next three months. Add into the chart the number of people it will take to produce those sales each week. Subtract the number of people you already have for each position, allow for employee turnover by adding in the number expected to lose. This will tell you the number of people you will need to hire for each position over the next three months. It will be accurate as long as forecasted sales are accurate.

Creating a staffing plan may be a project that you've never undertaken. Since I am mainly concerned with interviewing in this article, I will only highlight the key points. If you are interested in more information, you may contact the publisher.

Creating A Staffing Plan:

- Plan 3 months ahead

- Project your sales for 3 months

- Know the number of people you need

- Know the number needed for each department

- Know the length of training required

- START NOW

Also, you must be aware of any employee who could potentially be leaving. You do this simply by talking with each employee daily. Learn about their personal situation, spouse's work, children, pregnancy, etc. Don't forget: make certain that you know if they are happy with their work and their supervisors! If they aren't happy, you can bet that *she/he will be leaving!*

The key here is to always know your staffing levels! There is no reason, and definitely no excuse, why you shouldn't know the number of employees that you have in each department and if the possibility exist that you will need to replace an employee. You should always anticipate employee turnover. Unexpected turnover can cripple your business quickly.

Your customers don't want to hear that they received poor quality food or poor service because you lost a cook or server unexpectedly. It is unacceptable to make excuses to your customers! I know there are times when you lose an employee that is totally unexpected. It happens. However, if you work the plan laid out above, coupled with the system and processes in the next chapter, you will never be caught by surprise again without another employee ready to take the place of the one that just left.

In the words of my late, great friend:

"Proper Planning Prevents Piss-Poor Performance!"

■ Joe Elmore

CHAPTER 7

5 STEPS TO GREAT EMPLOYEES

If you've been in business for any length of time, I don't have to tell you how tough it is to hire the right people. Interviewing and hiring is one of the most critical task that we do as managers and it is not a task to be rushed through. Typically, we needed someone yesterday, so we bypass or overlook certain things about an applicant just to get a person that will fill the present need.

I know that in today's world of automation, large companies are resorting to using computers to automate the process of taking applications and filtering through those applications. Most corporations require applications to be filled out and submitted online through the internet. This achieves two things for the company: one, it cuts payroll cost because a human doesn't have to spend time filtering applications and, secondly, ensures that all applications are given equal assessment.

This application filtering process is needed for large businesses and it works well. However, in a small business, the personal touch can't be eliminated. Remember, we are in the people business and the personal filtering of applications and screening applicants is not only necessary, but is the desired method to start the hiring process.

After many years in managing restaurants, I developed a system to hiring great employees. The system worked – as long as we worked the system. Is it failsafe? No. The entire system is based on people and no system is failsafe when it is based on people because people are not failsafe. Was the system effective? Absolutely! Although I never actually put a pen and calculator to the statistics, I would say the system worked around 95% of the time.

I did note the following results. I was the opening manager for two different restaurants located across the street from the other. The two restaurants were with two different companies and were two different concepts. The first restaurant, after being in operation for ten years, still had over 10% of the original staff that I hired to open the restaurant when it was new. The second restaurant, after six years in operation, still had around 20% of the original opening crew.

Ground Rules

To make the System work, I laid some ground rules up front. I insisted that these ground rules be followed, with few exceptions. These ground rules were imperative and were simply created from my experiences and observations for the past several years.

I had made notes for years about the results of certain elements of interviewing and hiring and about employees in general. The Ground Rules were tough – but I had a reason for each one. I set the standard for the type employee that I needed working for me. Incorporated into those tough rules was the need for a certain type person that could produce high-quality food quickly and could provide a high level of service that my customers expected and paid to receive.

The Ground Rules that I set:

1. Applications are received at any time. In the restaurant business, most managers only want to take applications between 2 pm and 4 pm. That applicant that you turned away at 10 am may have been the employee that you needed.
2. All applicants are greeted by a manager. We are a people business and by greeting applicants we can put a face with the application and be people-oriented.

3. The first interview is always conducted by a non-hiring manager
4. The second interview is conducted by the hiring manager, the decision-making manager.

The Process to Better Employees

Over the course of several years, combining systems that I had used with my own processes, I created a hiring process. I call it the 5-Step Hiring System. At the time I set up the system, I had probably hired close to a thousand people. After opening the second new unit, as noted above, I became a traveling General Manager helping the company open other new units. Pressed for time with a heavy workload, I formalized the System and implemented it with my management staff. This results-driven hiring system paid off in many ways.

Benefits of the 5-Step Hiring System

- Structured: management knows each step that must happen
- Flexible: timelines for each step can be adjusted to the needs of the business and the applicant, but the steps remain in order
- Streamlined: very efficient
- Helps to hire better quality employees with less chance of getting a deadbeat

The 5 Step Hiring System

1. The **APPLICATION**

There is so much that can be learned from the application! You just have to know what to look for.

- Is the application fully completed? No blanks? I will not hire (or even interview) anyone who does not fill out the application completely. Why? This tells me that this person will not follow instructions.

- Longevity? Another standard of mine is that I won't interview a person who has not held a job for at least a year. There are a few exceptions, e.g., students, construction workers, etc.

- Legible handwriting. We have forms to fill out and lots of labels that we must be able to read.

2. **VERIFY APPLICATION**

- Anything can be written down on an application. So, I verify as much of the information as possible. I call the phone numbers on the application to validate that they work and are accurate, especially personal references. Verify and validate.

- In today's legal climate, it is hard to get a good reference check – but you can at least verify dates of employment, pay rate, and dependability. TIP: call the previous employer and ask to speak with a former co-worker. Also, be sure to talk to the applicant's personal references.

3. The **INTERVIEW**

- It is best to have a minimum of two interviews, one each with a different manager or department head. Each manager will see a different aspect of the applicant.

- If you are a sole owner of a business, then have two interviews but use a different set of questions each time. During the interviews, look for the criteria that you have set for the position.

- Here are four criteria that I look for no matter what position is being applied for:

a. Discipline: application completed fully, on time, no cell phone during interview

b. Longevity: with previous employment

c. Writing skills (also verbal skills)

d. Interest: does she/he ask questions pertinent to the position – not the pay

4.   The **APPLICANT'S TURN**

- Here is a step that is unusual, but it works. Many managers will be afraid to use this step, but I am open with my staff and not afraid of what they say about me.

- After completing the above three steps, if you feel really good about the applicant then move to step 4. You actually allow the applicant to come into your business and interview your staff to ask questions about the job. You see, in a people business, interviewing is a two-way street. We are looking to hire the applicant but we don't want to hire a person and a week later, the person realizes that this job is not for them. By following this step, you get a new employee that better understands the job and what the job entails.

- The applicant is allowed to ask any question of anyone who works there. This is his/her chance to interview you and your business. She/he is not paid – it's their own time. The applicant is not required to do this but it is a chance for him/her to find out if he/she really does want the job.

- Then, at the end, ask her/him what their thoughts are about the job. If you and the applicant agree, make the offer.

5.   **The OFFER**

- Be prepared! Give the new hire any necessary pre-employment paperwork, set the start date and time, the salary, and discuss what will occur on the first day of employment. Introduce the new person to other staff members and make her/him feel welcome immediately.

In this chapter, we have learned how to hire a great staff, how to treat employees, and maintain a great place to work without deadbeats.

Just to recap:

5 Steps to a Great Staff

- Hire lots of people
- Hire great people utilizing the 5 Step Hiring System
- Maintain a great work atmosphere
- Treat all employees with the utmost respect
- Take Action with deadbeats immediately, don't wait

Support Your Staff

Another key to maintaining a great staff is to support them in their work. If you, as a supervisor do not support your staff, why would you expect them to support you. Supporting your staff means many things:

- Ensure they have the needed tools available at all times. You can't expect them to flip hamburgers if they don't have a spatula to flip them with. If they don't have the tools they need, they feel that you really don't care about procedures
- If you have a female server who has a customer making uncool remarks to her and she ask you to get someone else to finish the table, what do you do?
- Dou you ensure that each employee gets their pay raise on time or shrug it off and say, "I sent it to corporate."
- If an employee comes to you wanting to talk to you about her/his schedule, do you say, "Let's do it", or do you tell them to see you at another time?

MY MOTTO:

If You Work For Me, I Work For You

CHAPTER 8

5 QUESTIONS
THAT TELL THE STORY

Can Your Candidate Tell The Story?

Here are five questions that I ask of job applicants or prospective employees and management candidates. These five questions will tell the story about that person. You should ask the same of anyone that you consider bringing into your business with you – your recruits. The reason: she/he will be representing you , your company, and your product.

By recruiting only "people" people, you will build a lasting business. Are these interview questions the only thing you need to know? Absolutely not but they are a good start. Weave them into your own set of question.

Five Questions

1. *Why did you leave your last job?* The response will tell me if the person worked well with people or if this person has a negative opinion of co-workers or supervisors.

2. *What three things would you consider as your strengths?*

3. *What three things would you consider as your weaknesses?* These two questions will tell me if the person knows themselves or even cares to know themselves. If he/she has been in the workforce for any period of time, they should be quick to answer these two questions. If they hesitate to answer or don't have real answers they will not help your business. If they don't really know themselves and believe in themselves, how can they really know a product and believe in that product enough to sell it. We've all heard that selling is just telling your story. Well, **if you can't tell me the story of *you* then you can't tell the story of my brand or product (sell).**

4. *What is a standard?* We all talk about standards but can you really define it? Can you give a definition of a standard – exactly what a standard is. Very few people can define exactly what a standard is in common sense terms. It makes you stop and think. If you can't define what a standard is and define it in terms that your people understand, then how can you enforce the standard?

5. *What is common sense?* Can you define what common sense is? In the people business, you need it and the people in your organization need it if your organization is to be successful.

Do I Want You On My Team? I'll find out.

Now, the first three questions above are self-explanatory. Each question is easy for the applicant to understand and easy for you to understand the reason why they are asked.

Let's talk about "common sense" for a bit. Common sense is definitely a trait that a leader or manager should have, at least in my opinion. You may disagree.

In my interviews where I have asked, "What is common sense?", I always get this look of disbelief as if, "Did he really just ask me that?" Of course, as you can imagine, I have gotten a variety of answers:

"Going inside when it's raining"
"Driving on the right side of the road"
"Knowing when to answer a question and when to keep quiet"
"Don't back-talk my momma"

In most cases, the applicant will take a moment or two before they answer, all the while scanning my face to try to figure out if I am serious. And I am. I am dead serious. Why?

If the person I am interviewing is a management candidate I want to know if he/she can "think on their feet" so to speak. There are many times as a manager or leader that we are faced with making a decision quickly. I want to see how this person handles this situation. The answer that's given is not always the most important part. What I look for is, did he/she stop to think before answering.

Thefreedictionary.com describes "common sense" as: sound practical judgement not based on any specialized knowledge or training. I think this is probably a pretty good answer. However, my answer is simply, "doing what's most practical for the situation".

In order to make you understand better without getting technical, I'll do as one of my applicants did. Rather than trying to give a good description of common sense, let me give you an example.

Many years ago while managing a steak and seafood restaurant, we were forced to buy a new flat-top range. All we really needed were the burners but we decided to buy a flat-top that also had an oven built under the flat-top burners. This would give us more usefulness without losing valuable space under the burners.

When the new equipment arrived, we set it into place where the old one had been located. It was management's thinking that the hook-ups were already there so it would be easy to get the new equipment operating. However, the question was raised as to the effectiveness of the location. Was it really the best place? Being a new General Manager who didn't know that managers made decisions and cook's lived by those decisions, I decided to ask the cooks where the best location would be. Where would be the best place to locate the burners and oven in relation to the menu and their work habits.

The cooks took a few minutes, discussed the situation, maybe argued among themselves a bit, but eventually told us where to locate the range. They explained their reasoning to us and that's where we located the range, even though we had to run new hook-ups. It just made sense and indeed helped to create a more efficient cook's line. Management thought a different location would be best but common sense said locate it where it would work best for the people who would be using it.

Another situation in which I believe common sense must prevail is when a customer has a problem with the product or service. Corporate rules will usually dictate how you should handle that situation, but common sense says that you solve the situation in favor of the customer. I think you will never go wrong by doing this.

In the next chapter, we will discuss standards and answer the question, "What is a standard?'

CHAPTER 9

DEFINITION OF A STANDARD

What is a "Standard?" How do you define "Standard?"

We constantly hear the word "standard". The word is used frequently in the business world to clarify corporate policies and procedures. In almost any training course you'll be trained on "standards". Yet, most people cannot give a definition of the word!

Why is that important? I believe that if you can't define what a standard is, then you can't establish standards and truly enforce them! By being able to tell a new employee what you mean when you say "standard", that employee, and every other staff member, will know precisely what you expect!

When you describe what a standard is, every staff member, including management will get the picture. When you enforce each standard, and expect each manager to enforce each standard, it will be almost impossible for a deadbeat to survive in your organization!

This is why it is so critical that you, and your staff, know what a standard is and be able to define the word "standard".

I was asked this question many years ago during a job interview. I had never really thought about the answer, until then. Since that time, I have woven the answer into my daily duties and definitely into my long-term planning. "Setting the standard" is expected as a leader, mother, father, teacher, or coach. The minister at our church is expected to set the standard. Setting the standard is easier when you have a clear definition of the word.

I also ask this question in my management candidate interviews. In the hundreds of interviews that I've conducted, I've probably had two people with the correct answer. In our society, we have few standards, mostly because very few people can actually define what is a standard. You must be able to not only define it, but be able to explain it to your staff.

What is a Standard?

Most people use the word "standard" in relation to rules and regulations, policies and procedures. And this is true. You'll hear managers say, "That is our standard." Or, "That is not to standard." So, before reading further, stop and take a minute to think about how you would describe or define "standard".

You may look up the word in the dictionary. Then, I'll challenge you to be able to explain the word or define the word to your employees in a manner that each will comprehend. For you see, this is the whole reason for this exercise. You must be able to tell, show, do and review. Right? You must be able to explain the word to your staff so that they understand what you mean. As I've said before, if we have an understanding now, there will be no misunderstanding later!

In the Merriam-Webster Dictionary and Thesaurus, 2007 Edition, the word "standard" is defined as follows: something set up as a rule for measuring or as a model to be followed. Now can you fully explain to your staff what is a standard? In my opinion, this definition could also fit a yardstick. Perhaps a measuring cup. A tire gauge. A blood pressure meter. It could fit many things.

I want you to be able to simply say, "This is my standard", and your staff will instantly know what you mean. Here is that definition.

A Standard is: "The least acceptable".

The absolute minimum that I will accept! I will accept no less than . . .
A standard is the very least that you will accept in the situation. In any situation, personal or business, we have to stop, think, and decide what the result will be for that situation. The decision we make then becomes the standard. That will be the least that we will accept! We then make sure that everyone in the project knows and understands what the "minimum acceptable" will be. The standard is enforced and reinforced through follow-up and coaching.

How do we put a standard into practice? It is always in the forefront of our mind. We teach it, we coach it, we achieve it! There are few, if any, compromises. The standard is simply "the way it is". I believe that when training, or learning a habit, it takes an ounce of theory but a pound of practice. This is how Olympians win gold medals!

An ounce of theory -
but a pound of practice!

CHAPTER 10

SUMMARY

Throughout this book, I have discussed leadership principles and management best practices in dealing with people. It was once said to me, " you manage things, you lead people".

In the context of this book, the title can be taken to have different meanings, depending upon how you read it. "It's Easier To Give Birth Than Resurrect The Dead" simply says that: it's easier to hire new employees than develop deadbeats into productive employees. Which path will you choose?

It is more noble to work with a laggard employee and turn a poor performer into a star employee. Too many times we, as managers, want to take the easy way out. I challenge you to do what's right.

I would be interested in hearing your stories of how you develop deadbeat employees. I am curious to know what you do to hire and maintain a great staff.

Talk to me through the publisher of this book: info@onpointpublishers.com

Anticipate. Adapt. Achieve.

ABOUT THE AUTHOR

Ted Duboise has worked in the restaurant industry for over 30 years. He has held various positions in the business. In almost every company, Ted was a Training Manager, responsible to train hourly employees and new Management Trainees. Ted still maintains his fervor for training and helping others to become a success.

www.ingramcontent.com/pod-product-compliance
Lightning Source LLC
Chambersburg PA
CBHW071412200326
41520CB00014B/3412